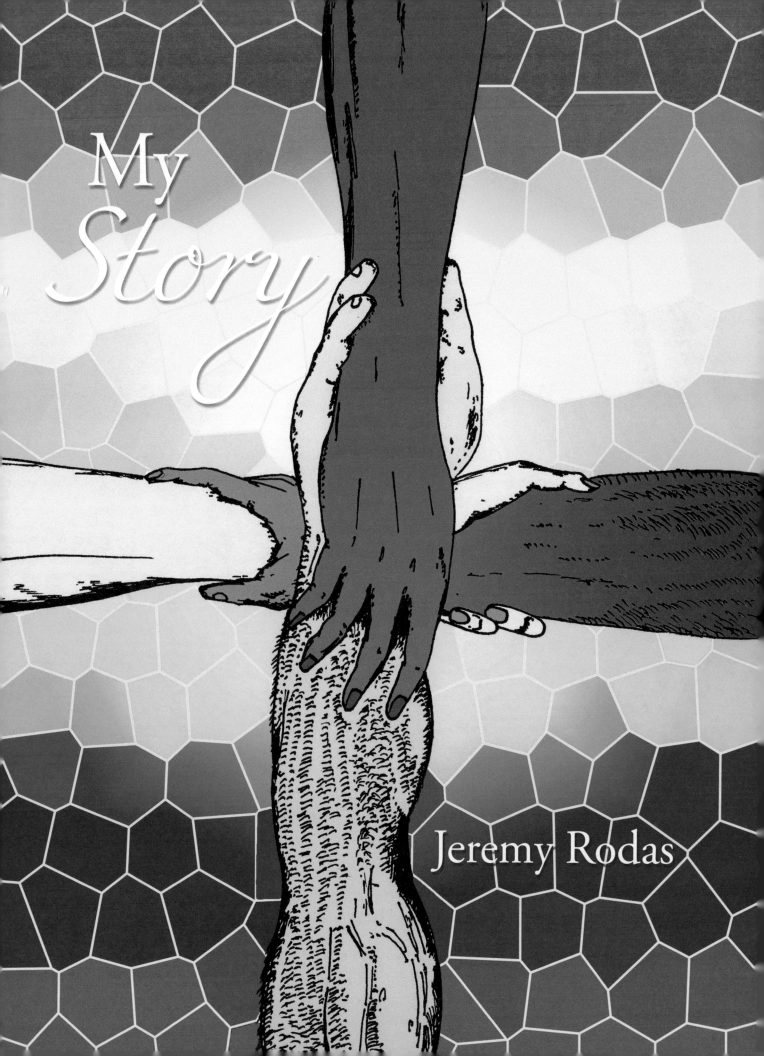

AuthorHouse™
1663 Liberty Drive
Bloomington, IN 47403
www.authorhouse.com
Phone: 1 (833) 262-8899

Because of the dynamic nature of the Internet, any web addresses or links contained in this book may have changed
since publication and may no longer be valid. The views expressed in this work are solely those of the author and do
not necessarily reflect the views of the publisher, and the publisher hereby disclaims any responsibility for them.

Any people depicted in stock imagery provided by Getty Images are models,
and such images are being used for illustrative purposes only.
Certain stock imagery © Getty Images.

This book is printed on acid-free paper.

ISBN: 978-1-7283-6829-0 (sc)
ISBN: 978-1-7283-6830-6 (e)

Print information available on the last page.

Published by AuthorHouse 08/04/2020

authorHOUSE®

Dedication

This book is dedicated to Shianna, Selena, Justin, Jason, Callie, Kyleigh, Zachias, and Mackenzie. You are wonderfully and fearfully made. You can do all things through Christ who strengthens you.

There once was a woman who was remarkably and wonderfully made.

Solomon 4:7

There once was a man who was
remarkably and wonderfully made.

PSALM 139:14

There once was a boy who was
remarkably and wonderfully made.

JEREMIAH 1:5

There once was a girl who was remarkably and wonderfully made.

Proverbs 31:29

There once was a family who were remarkably and wonderfully made.

There once was a woman who was sad.

13

There once was a man who was sad.

BOASTFUL

arrogant

controlling

COWARDLY

disloyal

There once was a boy who was sad.

CONFRONTATIONAL

EXISTENTIAL

Disorganized

frivolous

dishonest

There once was a girl who was sad.

Self

centered

vain

impolite

Over Critical

inconsiderate

19

There once was a family that was sad.

There once was a GOD that loved them.

Romans 5:8

23

There is a GOD that loves them.

LAMENTATIONS 3:22

There will always be a GOD that loves them and they are still remarkably and wonderfully made.

Psalm 100:5

27

Printed in the United States
By Bookmasters